ELIZABETH COLE

MY WAY TO GOOD MANNERS

Hello

Please

How are you?

May I help you?

Excuse me

I'm sorry

ILLUSTRATED BY
TATYANA KIM

"Good manners are just a way of showing other people that we have respect for them."

– Bill Kelly

Book by Elizabeth Cole

This book belongs to

....

....

Most of the time, Melissa is a very good child;
she's sweet and cheerful, and has a warm smile.
But sometimes, her good manners take flight
and, instead, her behavior becomes impolite.

She loves doing a handstand or a cartwheel,
but she doesn't wash her hands before a meal.
She likes eating salad with a sprinkle of lime,
but she eats with her mouth open every time.

Melissa loves to play with her hippo and her fox.
But she refuses to put them both back in the box.
And when her mom buys a hairband colored red,
Melissa doesn't say thank you, but grabs it instead.

At school, she is impatient to say what's on her mind;
she interrupts her friends, and that's not very kind.
She doesn't share her crayons even though she could.
This behavior makes her friends feel not very good.

She doesn't realize she is making others mad.
Until, one day, she felt lonely, rejected, and sad.
Melissa's classmates didn't invite her to fly a kite.
Frowning, they said, "Your manners just aren't right."

So, when Melissa got home, she sulked around.
She couldn't forget what happened at the playground.
With shiny tears in her eyes, she was as sad as can be.
She complained to her mom, "No one will play with me."

Melissa's mom wiped away her daughter's tears.
"Maybe you should get some manners, my dear.
Your friends may be hurt by your bad attitude.
They won't play with you if you act so rude."

"If you put yourself in their shoes, you will see
that a rude person is not who you want to be.
Show respect, care, and appreciation too.
Treat others as you want them to treat you."

Melissa wanted to follow her mom's good advice,
but she didn't quite know how to behave nice.
So, her mom suggested they make a good-manners list,
and write down the rules so they wouldn't be missed.

Melissa stuffed the list into her skirt pocket,
then she raced to the zoo as fast as a rocket.
But there was a long line-up outside the zoo.
She sighed, and wondered what she should do.

Mom said not to cut the line. "Look at the list instead."
"Ooh, I should try to be patient," little Melissa said.
She waited and waited and, surprisingly, felt fine.
She even let a mom and baby go ahead of her in line.

They reached the zoo cashier after a long while.
Melissa peered at her manners list, and put on a smile.
Very politely, little Melissa said with some ease,
"May I have tickets for me and my mum, please?"

When Melissa got tickets, she didn't know what to do.
So, she checked the list, and politely said, "Thank you."
She was very happy and excited to get into the zoo;
she got to see a roaring lion and a clumsy kangaroo.

Melissa helped the zookeeper when he accidentally fell.
She gave her helping hand and showed she cared as well.
But when the monkey started making fun of her every move,
Melissa said, "Mocking is something my list doesn't approve."

Melissa cared as well when she heard a whining sound;
a little boy had dropped his ice cream on the ground.
She patted him and assured him, "Everything will be fine.
Please, don't cry. I also have a treat. You can have mine."

The little boy was grateful that she wanted to share.
In return, he let Melissa play with his teddy bear.
Melissa was amazed and delighted as could be.
"If I am nice to others, others will be nice to me."

On their way home, Melissa saw a girl playing by a tree.
She told her, "I love your dress. It looks very pretty."
Melissa was overjoyed when the girl gave her a smile.
"Good manners are so cool, and can be part of my style!"

"With them, life seems more beautiful than ever.
So, I'll be polite and use good manners forever!"
When Melissa got home, she grabbed a broom,
and made her mom happy by cleaning her room.

At dinner, she placed her napkin across her knees.
She also learned to say, "Could you pass the salt, please?"
And when she accidentally spilled the tea from her cup,
she apologized and said, "I'm sorry. I will clean it up."

One day, Melissa left her manners list on the bed.
But, at school, "Good morning, everyone," she said.
And after class, Melissa knew exactly what to say.
"Bye, see you tomorrow." Then she added a wave.

At home, her mother was rocking the baby on her lap.
Melissa didn't shout while her brother was taking a nap.
Instead, Melissa showed she could be gentle and polite.
She kissed his tiny nose and said, "Love you, sleep tight."

Melissa brushed her teeth without Mom telling her to.
She was happy to hear, "Honey, I'm so proud of you."
When she got into bed, her list slipped to the floor.
Melissa just left it there; she didn't need it anymore.

GOOD MANNERS MATTER

Go here to get your "Match Manners" game

My dear little readers!

As you have already learned in this book, having good manners are crucial in everyday life.
Manners teach you to respect others and help others respect you.
I sincerely hope that this book has shown you some fun ways to be a nice person.
It will surely bring you many friends to play with and have a good time!

I would love to know your opinion about this book.
It will help me a lot while I write the next one. Yes, there will be another book!
There will be many more books in this series that are worth waiting for and reading!
Can you guess what challenges little Melissa might face next time?
How would she feel?

Share your ideas with me, and maybe you will find them in one of the following books!
Wouldn't that be awesome?! I'm so excited to hear from you! You can write to me at
elizabethcole.author@gmail.com or visit www.ecole-author.com
Your input means a lot to me!

You can leave your review of this book here:

With love,
Elizabeth Cole

Made in the USA
Middletown, DE
26 September 2023

39462722R00018